An Old Pic

BY KIM THOMPSON

A Little Honey Book

Crabtree Publishing
crabtreebooks.com

Tips for Teachers and Caregivers

This book supports early readers as they decode words to learn facts and gain knowledge about the world.

Before reading, make sure students understand the sound-spelling correspondences shown below as well as the high-frequency words shown on the next page. Introduce the vocabulary words.

During reading, provide feedback and encouragement as students sound out decodable words by blending individual sounds.

After reading, talk about and write about the topic. Share the information on page 16 to help students learn more.

Letters and Sounds

New:

Sound	Spelling
/k/	c
/n/	n

Review:

Sound	Spelling
short a	a
short i	i
/m/	m
/p/	p
/s/	s
/t/	t

Decodable Words

act, am, an, at, can, cap, cat, in, is, it, Mac, man, Nan, nap, pan, Pap, pic, pins, pit, Sis, sit, tan

High-Frequency Words

New: a, look, my, old, on, we

Review: had, I, run, the, this, was

Vocabulary Words

dad

family

mom

We sit.

We look at an old pic.

This is Pap at the pan.

Nan pins it on Pap.

The man in the cap is my **dad**.

Dad had Mac, a tan cat.

My **mom** can run.

My mom can act.

My sis had a nap.

Sis was in the pit.

family

Look at this pic.

I am in it.

This is my **family**.

Build Background Knowledge

Looking at old family photos is a good way to learn about history. Photos are important sources of information. They capture interesting facts about the moments in time when they were taken. Looking at details in photos, such as people's clothing, hairstyles, vehicles, technology, and surroundings, helps us learn about what life was like in the past.

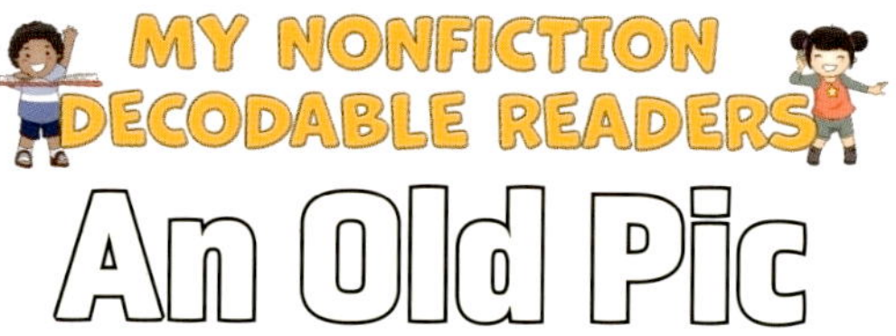

Written by: Kim Thompson
Designed by: Rhea Magaro
Series Development: James Earley
Educational Consultant: Marie Lemke, M.Ed.

Photographs: All images from Shutterstock

Crabtree Publishing

crabtreebooks.com 800-387-7650

Printed in China/012024/FE20231222

Published in Canada
Crabtree Publishing
616 Welland Ave.
St. Catharines, Ontario
L2M 5V6

Published in the United States
Crabtree Publishing
347 Fifth Ave
Suite 1402-145
New York, NY 10016

Library and Archives Canada Cataloguing in Publication
Available at Library and Archives Canada

Library of Congress Cataloging-in-Publication Data
Available at the Library of Congress

Hardcover: 978-1-0398-4427-8
Paperback: 978-1-0398-4509-1
Ebook (pdf): 978-1-0398-4586-2
Epub: 978-1-0398-4656-2
Read-Along: 978-1-0398-4726-2
Audio: 978-1-0398-4796-5